Self-Scoring IQ Tests for Children

Victor Serebriakoff

Honorary International President, MENSA

BARNES & NOBLE BOOKS
NEW YORK

This edition published by Barnes & Noble, Inc., by arrangement with Robinson Publishing Ltd.

ISBN 0-76070-163-6

Printed and bound in the United States of America

M 9 8 7 6 5 4 3

INTRODUCTION

First, a word of caution regarding all intelligence tests. These tests must be taken seriously, but not too seriously. The accepted view is that the only valid intelligence test is an individual test administered by a qualified educational psychologist. The development and validation of such a test involves thousands of hours of work by a team of highly trained experts. Publication generally would invalidate such a test.

Tests administered by nonprofessionals are less reliable, but self- or parent-administered tests can give a reasonably close first approximation of a child's IQ. However, whatever the outcome of the test, do not let your expectations be unduly raised or lowered. Providing that the parent is not "helping the child," the risk of underestimating a child's potential is more likely than overestimating it. If your child performs very poorly, you should consider a professional test.

Motivation is also an important fact when reviewing the results. The assumption behind every intelligence test is that the person taking the test is trying. If there is no motivation to succeed, then the test tells us little or nothing.

—Victor Serebriakoff
Honorary International President, MENSA
1995

THE TESTS

Two IQ tests are provided. They are both timed tests. These tests are suitable for children ages 7 through 14 who can read, write, and do arithmetic. They can be administered by supervisors or parents, who may read and explain the test, but it is intended that the children read the directions themselves. Generally, tests for children should be used with care and caution. Children's IQ or percentile ratings tend to remain fairly constant as they grow older, but there are exceptions. A very few children spurt or lag in IQ with time. It is best for each child to take a number of tests at intervals to get a better estimate. These tests measure *general intelligence* only. The child may have special abilities that seem inconsistent with his or her score. These skills should be watched for and developed.

The supervisor should adhere to the following rules:

1) Conduct the test at a time when you will be uninterrupted for an hour. Each child must have an eraser and a pencil.
2) If there is more than one child, photocopy the test form and make sure that each child's name is identified on the form he or she is using.
3) Tell the children to read the directions carefully. Then you should read them aloud slowly.
4) For older children (ages 12 and above), you can let them take the test by themselves when you give the signal to start.
5) With younger children, you may take them through the tests yourself, reading the test and repeating it. But be careful not to "help" or give the slightest indication of the answer verbally or by your expression. Do not respond to any question that can help with the answer and keep a poker face, since children are very quick at interpreting expressions. If you fail to observe these rules, you will be wasting both your time and the child's. So be strict.
6) Make sure all pencils are down at the end of the time (45 minutes).

Test begins here

TEST 1

Please add or subtract the following. For example: Adding 3 + 1 = 4, subtracting 3 – 1 = 2

Now write down the answers to the following:

1 6 + 2 =	**7** 21 – 4 =	**13** 31 – 16 =
2 9 – 5 =	**8** 29 – 8 =	**14** 41 – 40 =
3 6 – 2 =	**9** 14 – 6 =	**15** 31 – 27 =
4 9 – 1 =	**10** 18 – 6 =	**16** 26 – 18 =
5 8 + 21 =	**11** 22 – 7 =	**17** 29 – 12 =
6 4 – 3 =	**12** 38 – 14 =	

Read these incomplete sentences. There is a word left out. Underline (draw a line under) the word from the line below that will best go in the space.

Example: John sleeps in his _______.
table bed hat garden kitchen

bed is underlined because that is the best word.

Now you do it with the next ones. Underline the best word to go in the space.

18 Dogs _______ cats are pets.
or and with hamsters parakeets

19 John went _______ bed.
at by to on over

20 _______ are built for people to live in.
parks coats beds kennels houses

21 Apples are bigger _______ peas.
than as by much on

22 A peach is a kind of _______.
skin bush vegetable fruit seed

23 Fishermen use nets to _______ fish.
catch grab kill get have

24 John has _______ eyes.
tall ten one two eyebrows

25 Steam _______ hot.
makes is got has are

26 John stuck a _______ on a letter.
writing address stamps stamp

27 We use sugar to _______ our tea sweet.
got cause have make made

28 Pencils are used to _______ with.
write written right drawing writing

Here are some questions and some answers underneath. One answer is the best one. Underline the best answer.

29 What do we use to draw straight lines?
eraser sponges ruler desk compasses

30 Where do we go to catch a train?
station stop street town road

31 What takes a road over a railway line?
crane junction path cutting bridge

32 What do we open when we are out in the rain?
penknife book umbrella sunshade comic

33 What do we call the joint between the foot and the leg?
knee elbow ankle thigh toes

34 What do we call the bottom of a shoe?
tongue leather plastic sole nails

35 What do we call the part of an apple where the pips are?
middle core seeds skin peel

36 What do we call a room full of shelves of books?
shop kitchen library hall house

37 What is the middle of a wheel called?
hub axle pin rim tire

38 What do we use to tie our shoes?
string laces leather pins socks

39 Daisies, buttercups, and tulips. What do we call them?
bunch flowers fruit seeds garden

40 What collects the rainwater as it comes off a roof?
road pipe gutter tap drain

41 What do you call the two holes in your nose?
bridge entrance nostrils lobes gaps

Read these words.

dog <u>hat</u> <u>fat</u> mouse <u>mat</u> pot

<u>Hat</u>, <u>fat</u>, and <u>mat</u> are all underlined because they <u>rhyme</u>, or in other words, they end with the same sound.

Now you do it. Read these lines of words. Underline the <u>THREE</u> words in each line which rhyme.

42 say toe too mow far low

43 pay pat say pot hut hay

44 monk drink bank chunk sunk tank

45 meant mint dent pat tent fate

46 late bright rite light mate court

47 teak take leek bake speak oak

48 peat late tight fate right weight

49 muff bough how tough grow puff

A B C D E F G H I J K L M N O
P Q R S T U V W X Y Z

This is the Roman alphabet. Here are some questions about the order of the letters.

50 Which letter is midway between G and O? _______

51 Which letter is two after L? _______

52 Which letter is before one before C? _______

53 Which letter is after the letter which comes after N? _______

54 Which letter is before the letter that comes before J? _______

55 Which letter is the fourth after the letter which is midway between J and P? _______

56 Which letter is next after the fifth letter after D? _______

Now imagine each letter is on a card that can be moved.

57 Imagine that the first two cards with letters on them are changed over. Then the second two are changed over, then the next two, and so on all through right up to Z. Which letter will now come sixteenth? _______

58 Imagine that the fourth card, the eighth, the twelfth, the sixteenth, and so on are taken away. What will now be the sixth letter? _______

59 What would now be the two middle letters? _______

Read these words.

<u>long</u> wide <u>lengthy</u> tall <u>short</u> strong

<u>long</u> and <u>lengthy</u> mean the same thing but <u>short</u> means the opposite, so those words are underlined.

Now read each line of words and underline the best two words that mean the same and the word that most closely means their opposite.

60 start run jump begin finish walk

61 top end bottom side mountain summit

62 heavy weight weighty brilliant light feather

63 brilliant light lamp dim torch shining

64 come go approach farewell goodbye move

65 mute shouting music noisy deaf silent

66 growing contract climb shrink expand still

67 bliss smile misery grin anger joy

68 agreement quarrel meeting pact discussion deny

69 prosperous money impoverished millionaire affluent beggar

70 order arrange confusion combined muddle mixed

Here are a series of numbers. You have to find the <u>TWO</u> numbers that come next in the series from the line below. Underline the right two numbers.

3	6	9	12	15	<u>?</u>	<u>?</u>
1	9	<u>18</u>	4	3	<u>21</u>	

The numbers <u>18</u> and <u>21</u> are underlined because they come next in the series (the rule is add 3 each time).

That was easy. Now figure out the rule with these lines of numbers and underline the next two numbers from the list on the next page.

71

1	6	2	6	3	?	?
6	1	12	5	4	7	

72

128	64	32	16	?	?
10	12	4	3	8	9

73

2	5	4	7	6	?	?
3	7	9	8	1	6	

74

18	9	10	5	6	?	?
3	9	6	2	1	4	

75

3	4	6	7	9	?	?
9	8	10	6	2	12	

76

2	4	8	14	22	?	?
32	3	7	15	44		

77

2	3	30	31	310	?	?
2143	3110	3454	311	4343	211	

78

16	8	4	2	1	?	?
2/3	1/2	1/8	1/4	3/4	4	

79

2	3	4	3	4	?	?
3	5	10	4	2	1	

Read this line.

Coal black (rain snow mine hat white)

Coal is black and snow is white, so "snow" and "white" are underlined.

Now read this.

tablecloth table
(floor hat cup saucer knife)

A tablecloth goes on a table, so "cup" and "saucer" are underlined because a cup goes on a saucer.

Now underline the best TWO words in each line when you see the connection.

80 hen egg
(cow rabbit honey milk)

81 scales weight
(tape-measure length time thermometer volume)

82 skin man
(cat chicken fish snake fur)

83 old wrinkled
(smooth aged young happy father)

84 borrow lend
(give snatch take have send)

85 lake pond
(mountain hill sea land air)

86 cow herd
(school house sheep cat child)

You have only a dime, a quarter, and a 50-cent piece. A shop is selling glass marbles for 20 cents each and clay marbles for 15 cents each. You want to buy marbles spending just one coin and getting no change.

87 What is the most marbles you can buy for 50 cents? ________

88 How many can you get for 20 cents? ________

89 What is the smallest coin that will buy two sorts of marbles? _______

90 Using one coin to get the best value for your money, without getting back change, will you buy clay or glass marbles? Underline which.

clay glass

91 You can spend any two coins. What is the most marbles you can get? _______

Now try these.

Jack is four and Joan is seven. Both their birthdays are today.

92 Some years ago Joan was twice as old as Jack. How many years ago was it? _______

93 One day Jack will be three quarters of Joan's age. In how many years will that be? _______

94 When Joan was four times as old as Jack, how old was he? _______

95 When Joan is three times as old as Jack is now, how old will he be? _______

A cube which measures 30 inches each way is made up of a number of smaller cubes stuck together. They measure 10 inches each way. The large cube is painted black on the top and the bottom. The sides are all painted white.

Answer these questions.

96 How many small cubes have no paint on them? _______

97 How many have black paint on them? _______

98 How many have white paint on them? _______

99 How many have both black and white paint on them? _______

100 How many are painted on three sides? _______

END OF TEST. YOU SHOULD SPEND THE REST OF THE TIME CHECKING YOUR ANSWERS TO MAKE SURE THAT YOU GET AS MANY AS POSSIBLE RIGHT.

Answers are on page 10.

Answers begin here

ANSWERS TO TEST 1

Here are the answers to the questions. Each item is either right or wrong. One point for a correct answer. No penalties for errors. No half points.

1 8
2 4
3 4
4 8
5 29
6 1
7 17
8 21
9 8
10 12
11 15
12 24
13 15
14 1
15 4
16 8
17 17
18 and
19 to
20 houses
21 than
22 fruit
23 catch
24 two
25 is
26 stamp
27 make
28 write
29 ruler
30 station
31 bridge
32 umbrella
33 ankle
34 sole
35 core
36 library
37 hub
38 laces
39 flowers
40 gutter
41 nostrils
42 toe mow low
43 pay say hay
44 monk chunk sunk
45 meant dent tent
46 bright rite light
47 teak leek speak
48 late fate weight
49 muff tough puff
50 K
51 O
52 A
53 P
54 H
55 Q
56 J
57 O
58 G
59 M N
60 start begin finish
61 top summit bottom
62 heavy weighty light
63 brilliant shining dim
64 come approach go
65 mute noisy silent
66 contract shrink expand
67 bliss joy misery
68 agreement pact quarrel
69 prosperous affluent impoverished
70 confusion muddle order
71 6 4
72 8 4
73 9 8
74 3 4
75 10 12
76 32 44
77 311 3110
78 $\frac{1}{2}$ $\frac{1}{4}$
79 5 4
80 cow milk
81 tape-measure length
82 fur cat
83 young smooth
84 give take
85 mountain hill
86 child school
87 3
88 0
89 50 cent piece
90 glass
91 5
92 1
93 5
94 1
95 9
96 1
97 18
98 24
99 16
100 8

HOW TO WORK OUT YOUR CHILD'S IQ FROM THE SCORE

First, mark the test, giving one point for each question where the answer or answers are correct. Add up the correct answers (maximum 100). Look at the Key Number Table below. This gives a list of key numbers against each score. (The key number is 100 times the mental age in months for the score against it.)

1 Find the score nearest the child's score. Read off the key number opposite that score.

2 Calculate your child's age in months.

3 Divide the key number opposite the child's score by your child's age in months. Answer to the nearest whole number.

4 The answer is a rough estimate of the child's IQ.

5 If the number is over 175, take that as 175. The child has topped the charts.

EXAMPLE

A child aged 10 years and 3 months (123 months) scores 74.

The nearest score on the key table is 75, which gives a key number of 16900.

Divide this number by the child's age in months (123).

16900/123 = 137 to the nearest integer. This is the IQ of the child. It puts the child in the top tenth percentile for intelligence. The average IQ is 100.

KEY NUMBER TABLE FOR TEST 1

Score	Key Number (mental age in months × 100)
5	6600
10	7200
15	7900
20	8600
25	9400
30	10100
35	10700
40	11300
45	12000
50	12800
55	13600
60	14300
65	15100
70	15900
75	16900
80	18000
85	19100
90	20300
95+	21600

Test begins here

TEST 2

Read these directions very carefully. Then begin and work straight through. The first questions are very easy. Answer with care. The questions get harder as you work through the test. No one can do them all in the time provided. You have 45 minutes. You must work it out for yourself. Supervisors should not help the children and children should not ask them to.

Do not start the test until you are told or until the timing starts if you are testing yourself.

Start time ______________

Finish time ______________

(Test supervisor or child should make a note of the time and then start the test.)

1 6 + 3 =

2 8 – 5 =

3 6 – 2 =

4 9 – 3 =

5 6 + 21 =

6 6 – 3 =

7 11 – 4 =

8 25 + 8 =

9 14 – 6 =

10 17 – 4 =

11 18 – 9 =

12 29 + 16 =

13 28 – 17 =

14 27 – 16 =

15 25 – 23 =

16 27 – 12 =

17 23 – 11 =

Here are some sentences. There is a word left out where the lines ____________ are. Some of these words are the ones that were left out. See if you can see which words were left out in each sentence. Write them in over the lines.

Example:

Words: TO, CRIB, TABLE

Sentence: I like ______ sing.
Answer: I like __TO__ sing.

Sentence: A baby sleeps in a ______.
Answer: A baby sleeps in a __CRIB__.

The answers are here. Choose the right ones.

WASH AND TWO ARE SAIL TO HAPPY FRUIT SIT THAN IS MAKES DIN LOVE

18 Red ______ blue are colors.

19 Most days I go ______ school.

20 Men build ships to ______ in.

21 Giants are bigger ______ dwarfs.

22 An apple is a kind of ______

23 We have chairs to ______ on.

24 A butterfly has ______ wings.

25 Ice ______ cold.

26 Cows and sheep ______ farm animals.

27 Rain _______ the grass greener.

28 We use soap to _______ with.

Answer the following questions. The answers are all in the word list below. Write the correct answer in over the lines.

Example:

Answers FORK, HAT, KNIFE
Questions: What do you cut your food with? KNIFE

Answers

AIRPORT	TREE	KITCHEN
KEY	LACES	ESCALATOR
BLACKSMITH	WOOL	THERMOMETER
COMPASS	PIE	TRICYCLE
COAL MINE	STRING	FRUIT
HAT	JOKE	CHAIR

Here are the questions:

29 What do we use to draw a circle? _______

30 What are used to tie football boots? _______

31 Where do we go to catch an airplane? _______

32 What do we call a three-wheeled bike? _______

33 Who makes shoes for horses? _______

34 What fabric do we get from sheep? _______

35 What do we tie around a parcel? _______

36 What do we call the room where meals are cooked? _______

37 What instrument measures the temperature of a room? _______

38 Where does coal come from? _______

39 What do we use to unlock a door? _______

40 What do we call apples, lemons, and peaches? _______

41 What is a moving staircase called? _______

Look carefully at these words:

make, tool, bake, take, tall

Make, bake, and take all rhyme, so they are underlined.

Underline three words in each of the following sets which sound the same.

42 fit, tie, sit, seat, hit

43 book, bash, mash, hush, dash

44 head, hand, red, bread, hear

45 leak, mean, seek, beak, lean

46 book, round, look, took, bowl

47 clay, day, why, pray, clown

48 rule, fool, fowl, stool, roll

49 sigh, fig, dye, lie, mine

The alphabet is like this:

A B C D E F G H I J K L M N
O P Q R S T U V W X Y Z

Try to answer these questions. Write the answer on the dotted line.

50 What letter comes midway between H and P? _______

51 What letter comes right after S? _______

52 What letter comes right before Z? _______

53 What letter comes before the letter which comes before M? _______

54 What letter comes after the letter which comes after H? _______

55 Which letter is the 7th letter after the one which comes midway between E and S? _______

56 What letter comes just after the 7th letter after H? _______

57 Suppose the 1st and 3rd letters of the alphabet were switched, also the 2nd and 4th, then the 5th and 7th, then the 6th and the 8th and so on. Which letter would come 16th? _______

58 If the 3rd letter of the alphabet were crossed out, and also the 6th, 9th, 12th, etc., then which would be the 5th letter of the alphabet? _______

58 If the letters were crossed out as in the last question, what would be the last two letters? _______

Look carefully at these words:

dark, full, big, small, road, large

Big and large mean the same and small means the opposite. In the following sets of words, underline the two words which mean the same and also underline the word which means the opposite (you underline three words in each set).

60 dull, polish, gloomy, peer, bright, wind

61 happy, sad, below, pleased, shape, show

62 fast, feast, loom, slow, quick, look

63 loud, soft, touch, noisy, hard, tease

64 loser, eager, victor, keen, winner, take

65 tired, sleep, energetic, weary, feed, gone

66 open, door, wand, closed, shut, full

67 obese, thin, tiny, fat, tall, fen

68 still, left, motionless, moving, wound

69 pull, push, swing, take, tug, slice

70 stop, try, level, halt, start, stare

In these lines of numbers there is a rule which tells which number comes next. See if you can figure out the rule and then write in the next two numbers each time.

Example: 1, 2, 3, 4, ( ), ( )
Answer: 1, 2, 3, 4, (5), (6)

Now try with these:

71 1, 7, 2, 7, 3, ( ), ( )

72 128, 64, 32, 16, 8, ( ), ( )

73 7, 4, 9, 16, 11, ( ), ( )

74 26, 13, 14, 7, ( ), ( )

75 4, 5, 7, 8, 10, ( ), ( )

76 1, 3, 7, 13, 21, ( ), ( )

77 2, 3, 30, 31, 310, ( ), ( )

78 48, 24, 12, 6, 3, ( ), ( )

79 2, 4, 6, 5, 7, ( ), ( )

Look at these words:

coal, black
(dew, grass, twig, green, forest)

Coal is black and grass is green, so "grass" and "green" are underlined.

Next, look at these words:

hand, glove
(finger, face, foot, neck, arm, sock)

A glove is worn on the hand and a sock on the foot, so "foot" and "sock" are underlined.

Now you underline the best two words in each of the following lines:

80 roof, house
(hat, arm, show, head, finger)

81 time, clock
(room, radio, garden, baby, music)

82 fur, mink
(lion, wool, silk, sheep, gun)

83 old, antique
(gold, water, sand, precious, bad)

84 give, receive
(fetch, purchase, sell, carry, clean)

85 dwarf, giant
(estuary, stream, boat, river, land)

86 gaggle, geese
(owls, tigers, band, flock, sheep)

A man selling potatoes and carrots offers his potatoes at 10 cents a pound and his carrots at 15 cents a pound. I buy an exact number of pounds of vegetables and I pay with coins, receiving no change.

Now answer these questions:

87 What is the greatest weight of vegetables that I can buy with 50 cents? _______

88 What is the greatest weight that I can buy with 10 cents? _______

89 How much money will I need to buy two pounds of potatoes and two pounds of carrots? _______

90 What is the greatest number of pounds of potatoes that I can buy with one quarter? _______

91 If I can use one coin only, must I buy potatoes or carrots? _______

Now try these.

Jane is five years old.
Kay is nine years old.

92 How many years ago was Kay twice as old as Jane? _______

93 In how many years will Jane be two-thirds the age of Kay? _______

94 How old was Kay when she was three times Joan's age? _______

95 How old will Jane be when Kay is three times Jane's present age? _______

A number of cubes, each with an edge one inch long, are stuck together to form a solid cube with edges 3 inches long. Then this large cube is painted red on the top, and green on the bottom and four sides.

This is a cube:

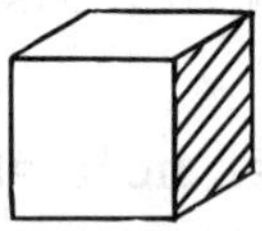

96 How many cubes are not painted at all? _______

97 How many cubes have red paint on them? _______

98 How many sides have green paint on them? _______

99 How many sides have both red and green on them? _______

100 How many cubes are painted on 3 sides? _______

Answers are on page 17.

✓ Answers begin here

ANSWERS TO TEST 2

Here are the answers to the questions. Each item is either right or wrong. One point for a correct answer. No penalties for errors. No half points.

(**1**) 9
(**2**) 3
(**3**) 4
(**4**) 6
(**5**) 27
(**6**) 3
(**7**) 7
(**8**) 33
(**9**) 8
(**10**) 13
(**11**) 9
(**12**) 45
(**13**) 11
(**14**) 11
(**15**) 2
(**16**) 15
(**17**) 12
(**18**) and
(**19**) to
(**20**) sail
(**21**) than
(**22**) fruit
(**23**) sit
(**24**) two
(**25**) is
(**26**) are
(**27**) makes
(**28**) wash
(**29**) compass
(**30**) laces
(**31**) airport
(**32**) tricycle
(**33**) blacksmith
(**34**) wool
(**35**) string
(**36**) kitchen
(**37**) thermometer
(**38**) coal mine
(**39**) key
(**40**) fruit
(**41**) escalator
(**42**) fit, sit, hit
(**43**) bash, mash, dash
(**44**) head, red, bread
(**45**) leak, seek, beak
(**46**) book, look, took
(**47**) clay, day, pray
(**48**) rule, fool, stool
(**49**) sigh, dye, lie
(**50**) L
(**51**) T
(**52**) Y
(**53**) K
(**54**) J
(**55**) S
(**56**) P
(**57**) N
(**58**) G
(**59**) Y, Z
(**60**) dull, gloomy, bright
(**61**) happy, sad, pleased
(**62**) fast, slow, quick
(**63**) loud, soft, noisy
(**64**) loser, victor, winner
(**65**) tired, energetic, weary
(**66**) open, closed, shut
(**67**) obese, thin, fat
(**68**) still, motionless, moving
(**69**) pull, push, tug
(**70**) stop, halt, start
(**71**) (7), (4)
(**72**) (4), (2)
(**73**) (64), (13)
(**74**) (8), (4)
(**75**) (11), (13)
(**76**) (31), (43)
(**77**) (311), (3110)
(**78**) ($1\frac{1}{2}$), ($\frac{3}{4}$)
(**79**) (9), (8)
(**80**) hat, head
(**81**) radio, music
(**82**) wool, sheep
(**83**) gold, precious
(**84**) purchase, sell

(**85**) stream, river
(**86**) flock, sheep
(**87**) 5
(**88**) 1
(**89**) 50 cents
(**90**) 2
(**91**) potatoes
(**92**) 1
(**93**) 3
(**94**) 6
(**95**) 11
(**96**) 1
(**97**) 9
(**98**) 45
(**99**) 12
(**100**) 8

THE RUSSELL TEST SCORE TABLES FOR TEST 2

Look under the heading of the child's age (whichever age is closest). Then read IQ against score.

M = Mensa level.

Age 7 years

Score	*IQ*	*Percentile*
7	79	10
9	83	13
11	87	20
13	91	27
15	95	37
17	99	47
19	103	58
21	107	68
23	111	77
25	115	84
27	119	90
29	123	94
31	127	96
33	131	98M
35	135	
37	139	
39	143	
41	147	
43	151	99M
45	155	
47	159	
49	163	
51	167	

Age 7½ years

Score	*IQ*	*Percentile*
7	78	9
9	82	12
11	86	18
13	90	25
15	93	32
17	97	42
19	101	52
21	104	60
23	108	70
25	112	79
27	116	86
29	119	90
31	123	94
33	127	96
35	130	98M
37	134	
39	138	
41	141	
43	145	
45	149	99M
47	153	
49	156	
51	160	
53	164	
55	167	

Age 8 years

Score	*IQ*	*Percentile*
7	78	9
9	81	10
11	85	16
13	88	21
15	92	30
17	98	37
19	99	45
21	102	55
23	105	63
25	109	73
27	112	79
29	116	86
31	119	90
33	123	94
35	126	96
37	130	98M
39	133	
41	137	
43	140	
45	144	
47	147	
49	151	99M
51	154	
53	158	
55	161	
57	164	

Age 8½ years

Score	IQ	Percentile
9	80	9
11	83	13
13	87	20
15	90	25
17	93	32
19	97	42
21	100	50
23	103	58
25	106	66
27	110	76
29	113	81
31	116	86
33	119	90
35	123	94
37	126	96
39	129	97
41	132	98M
43	136	
45	139	
47	142	
49	146	
51	149	99M
53	152	
55	155	
57	159	
59	162	
61	165	
63	168	

Age 9 years

Score	IQ	Percrentile
9	79	9
11	82	12
13	86	18
15	89	23
17	92	30
19	95	37
21	98	45
23	101	52
25	104	60
27	107	68
29	110	76
31	113	81
33	116	86
35	120	91
37	123	93
39	126	96
41	129	97
43	132	98M
45	135	
47	138	
49	141	
51	144	
53	147	
55	150	99M
57	153	
59	157	
61	160	
63	163	
65	166	
67	169	

Age 9½ years

Score	IQ	Percentile
9	79	9
11	82	12
13	85	16
15	87	20
17	90	25
19	93	32
21	96	40
23	99	47
25	102	57
27	105	63
29	108	70
31	111	77
33	114	82
35	117	87
37	120	91
39	123	94
41	125	95
43	128	97
45	131	98M
47	134	
49	137	
51	140	
53	143	
55	146	99M
57	149	
59	152	
61	155	
63	158	
65	161	
67	163	
69	166	
71	169	

Age 10 years

Score	*IQ*	*Percentile*
11	81	10
13	84	14
15	86	18
17	89	23
19	92	30
21	95	37
23	97	42
25	100	50
27	103	58
29	106	66
31	109	73
33	111	77
35	114	82
37	117	87
39	120	91
41	122	93
43	125	94
45	128	97
47	131	98M
49	134	99M (scores 49–73)
51	136	
53	139	
55	142	
57	145	
59	147	
61	150	
63	153	
65	156	
67	159	
69	161	
71	164	
73	167	

Age 10½ years

Score	*IQ*	*Percentile*
11	80	9
13	83	13
15	85	16
17	88	21
19	91	27
21	93	32
23	96	40
25	99	47
27	101	52
29	104	60
31	107	68
33	109	73
35	112	79
37	114	82
39	117	87
41	120	91
43	122	93
45	125	95
47	128	97
49	130	98M
51	133	99M (scores 51–77)
53	136	
55	138	
57	141	
59	144	
61	146	
63	149	
65	151	
67	154	
69	157	
71	159	
73	162	
75	165	
77	167	

Age 11 years

Score	*IQ*	*Percentile*
11	79	9
13	82	12
15	84	14
17	87	20
19	89	23
21	92	30
23	95	37
25	97	42
27	100	50
29	102	55
31	105	63
33	107	68
35	110	76
37	112	79
39	115	84
41	117	87
43	120	91
45	122	93
47	125	95
49	127	96
51	130	98M
53	132	99M (scores 53–81)
55	135	
57	137	
59	140	
61	143	
63	145	
65	148	
67	150	
69	153	
71	155	
73	158	
75	160	
77	163	
79	165	
81	168	

Age 11½ years

Score	IQ	Percentile
11	79	9
13	81	10
15	84	14
17	86	18
19	88	21
21	91	27
23	93	30
25	96	40
27	98	45
29	101	52
31	103	58
33	105	63
35	108	70
37	110	76
39	113	81
41	115	84
43	117	87
45	120	91
47	122	93
49	125	95
51	127	96
53	130	98M
55	132	
57	134	
59	137	
61	139	
63	142	
65	144	
67	146	99M
69	149	
71	151	
73	154	
75	156	
77	158	
79	161	
81	163	
83	166	
85	168	

Age 12 years

Score	IQ	Percentile
13	81	10
15	83	13
17	85	16
19	87	20
21	90	25
23	92	30
25	94	34
27	97	42
29	99	47
31	101	52
33	104	60
35	106	66
37	108	70
39	111	77
41	113	81
43	115	84
45	118	88
47	120	91
49	122	93
51	125	95
53	127	96
55	129	97
57	131	98M
59	134	
61	136	
63	138	
65	141	
67	143	
69	145	
71	148	
73	150	99M
75	152	
77	155	
79	157	
81	159	
83	162	
85	164	
87	166	
89	169	

Age 12½ years

Score	IQ	Percentile
13	80	9
15	82	12
17	84	14
19	87	20
21	89	23
23	91	27
25	93	32
27	96	40
29	98	46
31	100	50
33	102	55
35	104	58
37	107	68
39	109	73
41	111	77
43	113	81
45	116	86
47	118	88
49	120	91
51	122	93
53	124	94
55	127	96
57	129	97
59	131	98M
61	133	
63	136	
65	138	
67	140	
69	142	
71	144	
73	147	
75	149	
77	151	99M
79	153	
81	156	
83	158	
85	160	
87	162	
89	164	
91	167	
93	169	

Age 13 years

Score	IQ	Percentile
15	82	12
17	84	14
19	86	18
21	88	21
23	90	25
25	92	30
27	94	34
29	96	40
31	99	47
33	101	52
35	103	58
37	105	63
39	107	68
41	109	73
43	111	77
45	114	82
47	116	86
49	118	88
51	120	91
53	122	93
55	124	94
57	126	96
59	129	97
61	131	98M
63	133	
65	135	
67	137	
69	139	
71	141	
73	143	
75	146	
77	148	
79	150	99M
81	152	
83	154	
85	156	
87	158	
89	161	
91	163	
93	165	
95	167	

Age 13½ years

Score	IQ	Percentile
15	81	10
17	83	13
19	85	16
21	87	20
23	89	23
25	91	27
27	93	32
29	95	37
31	97	42
33	99	47
35	102	55
37	104	60
39	106	66
41	108	70
43	110	73
45	112	79
47	114	81
49	116	86
51	118	88
53	120	91
55	122	93
57	124	94
59	126	96
61	128	97
63	130	98M
65	132	
67	134	
69	136	
71	139	
73	141	
75	143	
77	145	
79	147	99M
81	149	
83	151	
85	153	
87	155	
89	157	
91	159	
93	161	
95	163	

Age 14 years

Score	IQ	Percentile
15	80	9
17	82	12
19	84	14
21	86	18
23	88	21
25	90	25
27	92	30
29	94	34
31	96	40
33	98	45
35	100	50
37	102	55
39	104	60
41	106	66
43	108	70
45	110	76
47	112	79
49	114	82
51	116	86
53	118	88
55	120	91
57	122	93
59	124	94
61	126	96
63	128	97
65	130	98M
67	132	
69	134	
71	136	
73	138	
75	140	
77	142	
79	144	
81	146	99M
83	148	
85	150	
87	152	
89	154	
91	156	
93	158	
95	160	

A FEW FINAL WORDS FROM THE AUTHOR

When you have completed this test and estimated your child's IQ, you may want to have a supervised test given by an educational psychologist. The test will cost you about $250.00.

You may also decide to apply to Mensa, which arranges less expensive tests for applicants. I am the Honorary International President of Mensa, a club whose members score at the top 2% on an intelligence test.

Mensa addresses are as follows:

American Mensa Inc.
2526 East 14th Street
Brooklyn, NY 11235-3992
USA

Mensa House
Saint John's Square
Wolverhampton WV2 4AH
UNITED KINGDOM

All other countries, please forward inquiries to:

Mensa International
15 The Ivories Northampton St.
London N1 HY
UNITED KINGDOM